Pebble® Plus

Animal Offspring

Tigers and Their Cubs

Revised Edition

by Margaret Hall

CAPSTONE PRESS
a capstone imprint

Pebble Plus is published by Capstone Press,
1710 Roe Crest Drive,
North Mankato, Minnesota 56003
www.mycapstone.com

Library of Congress Cataloging-in-Publication Data
Names: Hall, Margaret, 1947- author. Title: Tigers
and their cubs : a 4D book / by Margaret Hall.
Description: Revised edition. | North Mankato,
Minnesota : an imprint of Capstone Press, [2018] |
Series: Pebble plus. Animal offspring | Audience:
Age 4-8. | Includes bibliographical references and
index. Identifiers: LCCN 2017037874 (print) | LCCN
2017056622 (ebook) | ISBN 9781543508666 (eBook
PDF) | ISBN 9781543508260 (hardcover) | ISBN
9781543508383 (paperback) Subjects: LCSH: Tiger
cubs--Juvenile literature. | Parental behavior in
animals--Juvenile literature. Classification: LCC
QL737.C23 (ebook) | LCC QL737.C23 H334 2018 (print)
| DDC 599.75613/92--dc23 LC record available at
https://lccn.loc.gov/2017037874

Editorial Credits
Gina Kammer, editor; Sarah Bennett, designer;
Morgan Walters, media researcher;
Katy LaVigne, production specialist

Photo Credits
Getty Images: CHARLY TRIBALLEAU, 9;
Shutterstock: Africa Studio, 13, Anan Kaewkhammul,
11, left 20, chanyut Sribua-rawd, right 20, Cynthia
Kidwell, Cover, Dennis Jacobsen, 5, George Lamson,
15, Julian W, 17, neelsky, right 21, otsphoto, left 21, Raj
Wildberry, 3, Volodymyr Burdiak, 19, Xseon, 7

Note to Parents and Teachers

The Animal Offspring set supports national science
standards related to life sciences. This book describes
and illustrates tigers and their cubs. The images
support early readers in understanding the text.
The repetition of words and phrases helps early
readers learn new words. This book also introduces
early readers to subject-specific vocabulary words,
which are defined in the Glossary section. Early
readers may need assistance to read some words and
to use the Table of Contents, Glossary, Read More,
Internet Sites, Critical Thinking Questions, and Index
sections of the book.

Table of Contents

Tigers

Tigers are mammals.

Tigers are large cats
with whiskers.

A female is a tigress.

Young tigers are cubs.

A male tiger mates
with a tigress.
The male tiger leaves
before the cubs are born.

Tiger Cubs

A tigress gives birth to two

or three cubs.

The cubs drink milk

from her body.

Cubs are born blind and deaf.

They can see and

hear after two weeks.

Growing Up

Cubs rest during the day.

They grow quickly.

The tigress licks the cubs

to clean them.

She keeps them safe.

The tigress teaches the cubs
to hunt and find food.

Cubs live with their mothers
for about two years.
Then each cub leaves
to find its own home.

Watch Tigers Grow

birth

adult after about four years

21

Glossary

birth—to be born; a tigress gives birth to a group of cubs

blind—being unable to see; tiger cubs are born with their eyes closed; their eyes open after two weeks

deaf—being unable to hear; cubs can hear after two weeks

mammal—a warm-blooded animal that has a backbone and hair or fur; female mammals feed milk to their young

mate—to join together to produce young

tigress—an adult female tiger

whisker—one of the long, stiff hairs near the mouth of an animal

Read More

Esbaum, Jill. *Tigers.* Explore My World. Washington, D.C.: National Geographic Partners, LLC, 2016.

Macheske, Felicia. *Striped Stalkers.* Guess What. Ann Arbor, Mich.: Cherry Lake Publishing, 2017.

Thomas, Isabel. *Lion vs. Tiger.* Animal Rivals. North Mankato, Minn.: Heinemann Read and Learn, 2018.

Internet Sites

Use FactHound to find Internet sites related to this book.

Visit *www.facthound.com*

Just type **9781543508260** and go.

 Check out projects, games and lots more at
www.capstonekids.com

Critical Thinking Questions

1. Why do the cubs need to learn to hunt?

2. Tigers are mammals. What does the word "mammal" mean?

3. Why is it important for the mother to care for her cubs before they are two weeks old?

Index